Dave Gaskill's World

Cartoons from *Today*

DAVID GASKILL

CHAPMANS

For Irene

Chapmans Publishers Ltd
141–143 Drury Lane
London WC2B 5TB

First published by
Chapmans 1992

© David Gaskill 1992

The right of David Gaskill to be identified
as the author of this work has been asserted
by him in accordance with the Copyright,
Designs and Patents Act, 1988

ISBN 1–85592–638–5

Printed and bound in
Great Britain by
Clays Ltd, St Ives Plc

Foreword

by Sir Geoffrey Plumhampton

'Would you write a humorous Foreword for us?' the
publishers asked me, the day before this book went to
press.

'What do I know about politics, dear boy?' I asked in
return.'

'Not a lot, but we've only just remembered.'

'But what shall I write about?'

'Oh, press freedom and public figures,' they suggested.

'You mean whether seedy deeds – sorry, financial advice
– in private should be made public?'

'Yes, that sort of thing.'

'Or,' I said, warming to the task, 'shameful acts done in
public should be kept private?'

'Sorry . . .?'

'Oh, never mind. I must insist on complete anonymity,
you understand. There is a part of my life that I've no wish
to be made public. Same again?'

'You can rely on complete discretion,' they purred.

Now this, I must admit, was a great relief. 'Can you
imagine what would happen if my wife, child and mistress
found out I was a Member of Parliament? The shame is
too ghastly to contemplate. Mum's the word, old boy,' I
told them. 'Just in case.'

'Suits you,' they said.

Sir Geoffrey Plumhampton,
Annie's Bar,
House of Commons,
London SW1

Preface

Dave Gaskill's world is a parallel world to the one we know. The same dramatic events, scandals and day-to-day routines are played out by the same cast of kings, queens, bearers of high office and the merest of mortals.

However, the rules are changed – gravity need not apply, captains of industry are not compelled by their innate sense of fair play to restrict themselves to meagre 300 per cent pay increases, England's cricketers can win, Gazza can sing and British Rail arrive on time (no, perhaps that is stretching credulity too far).

In this alternative world Gaskill can imprison tall Texans in the Tower, no doubt with the royal approval of real-life monarchs.

Economic Norm can be helped as he wrestles forlornly but stubbornly with the recession (what recession)?

A suitable desert island can be found where Ministers of Fun can recharge their battery-operated telephones.

A few deft strokes of the pen and Colosseum-sized Pavarotti is reduced to sylph-like proportions.

Even a quiver can be put into John Major's stiff upper lip and a further bizarre excuse can be added to British Rail's remarkable collection.

Today's cartoonist has created this wry and lively imaginary world from material freely available on our sometimes dark and desperate orb.

But, can he spell? Well I must say, as his editor, that things have improved since he enrolled for the 'Dan Qayal corispondense coarse for coret speling'.

Though the Queen is reported to have no immediate plans to knight him, she is prepared to provide safe accommodation in the Tower . . . alongside any tall Texans who rock the royal boat.

Martin Dunn,
Editor,
Today

1   A Mad Old World

In 1992, surveys revealed our only too human shortcomings . . .

'It wasn't *that* funny, surely?'

. . . And our little idiosyncracies . . .

'Gosh, is that ten dinners with the same date?'

In 1992, surveys even revealed our failures . . .

. . . In fact, the year made us only too aware of the ticking of the clock

'I'll give it to you straight – you may have left it a bit late'

'Politically Correct' thinking, imported from America, threatened to become a bore during the year

'. . . And this little piggy changed his name by deed poll to avoid causing offence'

Scaling Everest became as mundane as a trip to the Council tip (and with just as much rubbish to clamber through)

'Typical – you don't see one for hundreds of years then along come thirty!'

1992 also saw some bizarre new gift ideas . . .

'So I goofed – but it's the thought that counts, honey'

. . . And equally bizarre court cases after a man was alleged to have had a pash for a dolphin

'I'd just like you to know I'm not that sort of fish'

. . . There were also some bizarre conferences during the year . . .

'Cosmonaut Boris Ivanoff could not be with us today but happily his son is here to talk about the side effects of sex in space'

. . . But still, we managed to hold on to lofty ideals

'What's a three thousand year wait for a dressing to be changed worth?'

2 The Royal Year

The custody of the horses now settled, a divorced
Princess Anne was able to play 1992's full
field (or pond) . . .

This isn't working, Mummy

Dave Gaskill sees me as a frog. Well, that's the way he
drew me in a recent cartoon. A frog, indeed!

It's all because I wrote about the Royal Family and
Gaskill saw it as a way of showing what revenge members
of that embattled family would like to take on authors.
Well, if they wanted to reduce me to the size of a frog
waiting for some Prince Charming to come along and
rescue me, what would the Windsor dynasty want to do
to a cartoonist like Gaskill?

They could always force him to paint the railings
round Buckingham Palace (it takes eight weeks at a
time), but then the tourists would just get some of the
funniest graffiti ever written – no doubt something based
on the line that Fergie, Mark, Diana, etc., used to live
here.

They could always throw him in the Tower. He'd only
borrow a pen and a slip of paper to write down his last
wishes and turn it into a drawing, perhaps of a Royal
running around headless . . . a little like some of the
officials at Buckingham Palace in recent crises.

As you can see from this book, there's nothing
headless about Gaskill's characters.

Penny Junor

. . . Until Steve Wyatt, a handsome American playboy, began to fuel rumours about the Yorks

The Queen was not amused by the Texan connection when the Yorks split up . . .

'I guess a guy sho' has made it socially when he's detained during Yo Majesty's Pleasure, Ma'am'

. . . And nor were others when Andrew and Fergie finally made their move

'Are they planning a "Changing of the Partners" ceremony?'

It was essentials first when the Yorks went their separate ways . . .

'Well that's the holiday brochures away, Ma'am – we'll be back later for the furniture'

. . . Provisions for the royal purse would have to be made

'Surely you don't begrudge the poor girl a proper settlement, Philip?'

Where on earth can her estranged parents-in-law go that globe-trotting Fergie hasn't been?

'We want somewhere our daughter-in-law isn't, hasn't been and is unlikely to be'

The royal separation provoked some funny business, as Fergie put a bag over her head on a flight across the Atlantic

'I'm afraid the Duchess has just left on another promotional assignment, Your Highness'

Buy! Buy! Buy! As Andrew and Fergie parted company, many wondered whether their house, dubbed 'South York', would be put up for sale . . .

'I know it's rather a delicate time, Your Highness, but I was wondering if we could have first refusal on the property?'

. . . Meanwhile cracks were appearing in Prince Charles' marriage. He failed to join his wife on a visit to that lovers' shrine, the Taj Mahal

'Contrary to press reports, we have reason to believe that the Prince has been in the vicinity'

Separate holidays and swarms of paparazzi around his relatives were beginning to take their toll on the Prince . . .

'Pssst – saucy poolside photos'

. . . There was endless speculation about the state of his marriage

'You don't suppose there's any threat of being cited as co-respondents?'

'That book' by Andrew Morton – the most talked about volume of 1992. But was anyone happy?

The storm over the Andrew Morton book caused Princess Diana to seek solace with friends

'I think it's the royal seal of disapproval!'

What did Prince Charles make of all the revelations about his marriage? Perhaps he was first bemused . . .

. . . And then angry

That book again – but was Prince Charles in a forgiving mood?

The fall-out from the Princess Di affair meant that some royal telltales lost their jobs, though they did get to keep their heads

'Qualifications? Well, discretion for a start . . .'

After all her recent family troubles, Her Majesty can only live in hope . . .

. . . And perform one's duty, of course, even if that means addressing the European Parliament

'We think we've got her speeches right now – a nice mix of European culture and traditional jingoism'

Feeling the pinch? The royals wanted to claim for fencing their Balmoral estate against hungry deer

'Spare some change for those more fortunate . . .'

There's only one certain way to avoid becoming a suitable subject for Dave Gaskill and that's not to do anything that you do not want to read about in the papers. As a reporter, I thought I would always be safe from the cartoonist's sword. Then my own name was in the headlines, specifically over my book *Diana: Her True Story*. Suddenly I became a target for Gaskill who could have given this book the title *Gaskill: My True Characters*.

But you learn quickly about any objections you might have at the way cartoonists portray you. The next day they can make you look even worse. The only way I can get back at him is to be asked by *Today* newspaper to review this book. The trouble is that two of his recent cartoons about me take pride of place in our living room!

Andrew Morton

3　International Incidents

Communism finally gave up the ghost in 1992, but the queues lingered on

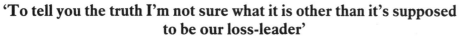

**'To tell you the truth I'm not sure what it is other than it's supposed
to be our loss-leader'**

The old Soviet Union's difficulties did not apply to a shortage of weapons. In fact, they had too many . . .

'Honey, sometimes I jest think you spoil those kids'

. . . Everyone could have their own rocket!

'It's set on Washington – how d'you reprogramme it for next-door-but-one?'

With Boris Yeltsin at the helm in Moscow, the world seemed a safer place – perhaps . . .

. . . Unless your name was George Bush. His dining habits at a banquet in Japan threw up a frightening scenario along with his dinner

'We've fed him the whole menu and he's still in there, dammit!'

For a time, George Bush's international problems were overshadowed by the riots in Los Angeles. Strong nerves – and doors – were required

1992 saw a new Aussie prime minister, the pom-punching Paul Keating, who liked being beaten
by England in the World Cup cricket even less than he liked royal protocol

'Politically naive and inept he may be, but unsporting he's not'

4   Commercial Breaks

The commercial properties of his telephone speaking apparatus would surely not have been lost on its inventor . . .

'You mean all it does is make a ringin' noise, you shout down it an' billions of pounds roll in? Go on, Mr Bell, pull the other one'

. . . Nor on BT as it continued to pile up huge profits in 1992

Like BT, the oil companies continued to do very nicely, thank you, during the year – more than can be said for their customers

'Is that a phone box or a petrol station?'

Short of money, Chancellor? As the recession bit, the banks showed that they know how to make us shorter

'What more could I do, for godsake – they charge you £35 for the mildest of rebukes!'

Criticized for their high-handed attitude, and even higher charges, the banks were keen to show that they listened . . .

'We fully understand your grievances, sir – now, if you'd care to go to our Slapped Wrist Department'

. . . The housing market fell even further in 1992, making Grimm reading to be sure

'I don't know what fairy tales you've been reading, lady – we're just here to repossess you'

Rumours had it that Rolls-Royce was up for sale – and that everyone would be sacked before being re-employed . . .

'I suppose you can expect a few cock-ups in 34,000 jobs, Mr Ex-Chairman – now stop snivelling and get out of my office!'

... In fact, Rolls's troubles touched many a sore spot

'Your Lordship's not taking the news very well, pardon me for saying'

Recessionary tales – there are still a few rich around, mind . . .

'Ah, the sheer enthusiasm of youth'

... Particularly the captains of some privatized industries who enjoyed huge pay rises during the year

'I've just been privatized!'

High unemployment was a price worth paying if that meant squeezing out inflation, according to Chancellor Norman Lamont

'I used to be just a worthless itinerant, but now I'm a price worth paying'

A takeover battle threatened hard times for the Listening Bank. There were rumours that a takeover would mean job cuts

'Psssssst! Gizzajob!'

The future of Lloyd's was in doubt as scores of 'Names' protested that massive cash calls would bankrupt them

'Oh, well – there goes the neighbourhood'

Even in hard times, there's someone worse off than you. Gerald Ratner's memorable remark about some of his products rebounded when his jewellery business ran into trouble

'It may be a bit of crap to you, Michelle, but it set me back forty quid and Gerald Ratner 17 million'

5   The Big Splash

Robert Maxwell's demise sent the rumour mill overboard. One was that he and a minion had been involved in spying with the Israelis

Captain Bob was famous for scattering writs like confetti. The things said about him after Mirrorgate would have sent the litigious tycoon off his rocker (or boat)

'Those are just the writs – we'll be along with the first edition later'

After his big splash, could Captain Bob bluff his way into new ventures? . . .

. . . Or would he be up to his old tricks again?

'We can't ask for his halo back – he's used it as collateral'

Captain Bob liked to keep tabs on his underlings by bugging their offices . . .

'It's such a relief to have an unbugged conversation at last'

. . . But others preferred to keep quiet about the old rogue's activities

6   And the Winner is . . . zzzzz

At the beginning of 1992 the Tories were despondent about their election chances

Labour went into the New Year full of vim at the prospect of a spell in government

'Thank god Wales only win every blue moon'

As the election got underway, the going got tough . . .

'Yuk! This must be the smear campaign they're all talking about!'

. . . Unlike Paddy Ashdown, John Major had no time for romance

'If it's not from Norma we'd better get the court injunctions ready'

Imaginative party political broadcasts about the NHS caused a furore during the election . . .

'Oh stop whining, Waldegrave, you know we Conservatives would never stoop to using
professional actors'

. . . Many thought the promises of more money for everything were even more imaginative

'Ah, I see you asking yourself, who's going to pick up the tab for all these giveaways?'

As the parties ran neck and neck in the election polls, spin doctors and image-makers got to work on their charges

Early in the year, England just managed to beat their opponents in the World Cup cricket series after a rule change – a point not lost on cricket-mad John Major

As the election neared, party publicity machines ran at full throttle . . .

'. . . There's this real scary scene involving a huge and hideous budget deficit'

. . . And professionals were on hand to sooth the occasional fevered brow

'Well, it seems that last question completely floored Sir Geoffrey – now, is there a spin doctor in the house?'

Just who would form the next government was a cliffhanger until the last moment . . .

'I think privately he's providing for the possibility of defeat'

. . . Fuelled by poll and counter-poll

'No need for despondency, Prime Minister – we're still in there, marginally
ahead of bankers and estate agents'

Many people thought that 1992's election would mean a hung parliament

'It might only be a 4% swing to you but it means another nine months' job security to me!'

Vote for Wally? By the end of the election, many weary voters wouldn't have given a XXXX for any other politician

'Sometimes, Rover, I think I'm becoming cynical'

Poll-bashed and manifesto-mugged, on 9 April the electorate finally had their say . . .

'Hello . . . er . . . I don't know if it's convenient, but
I've . . . er . . . changed my mind again'

. . . The result brought elation to some

'John dear, it's over, try and relax'

10 April 1992 – despair for the losers . . .

'Relive the glorious past, sir – pre-election polls'

. . . And a surprise for the winners

'Nothing personal, sir – I was just expecting somebody else'

Dawn on 10 April 1992 – and David Owen's SDP had vanished

'Well, actually it's a whole party gone missing – the SDP'

The election over, it was back to boring old life

'Ignore him – it's just a post-election phase they go through'

7 Sporting Times

Early in the year, Beefy Botham was torn between stage and side-screen when he delayed touring Australia because he was playing the king in a pantomime . . .

'A simple "owzat" sufficed in my day'

. . . But Ian still did his bit for Queen and Country when in Australia someone played Her Majesty in drag

Another recent World Cup. It's a rough old game, rugby – particularly for some officials of the series who were attacked by a French coach . . .

'Now, if you thought the French match was hazardous to officiate . . .'

. . . And the Welsh were losing on and off the field

Gazza had a few rough moments on his way to becoming a big Italian soccer star . . .

'Look son, nobody said being a Gazzalike was going to be easy'

. . . In fact, he became a bigger star than the Italians would have liked

'They gave up trying to slim him and retrained him as a tenor'

Concern over riding accidents prompted calls for the young princes to keep their hats on . . .

'Call me a sentimental old monarchist but it's nice to see the young princes at least wearing hats'

... And Mike Tyson's courtroom drama suggested that he might have done better to keep his *pants* on

Summer's here at last – and there's nothing like Wimbledon for the camaraderie of the queues . . .

**'Wake up, 'arry, we've just 'ad respectability thrust upon us – we've become part of a
Wimbledon queue'**

. . . And the extraordinary farmyard sounds made by some contestants

'Try it – just close your eyes and my word, you could almost be at Wimbledon eating strawberries'

The Olympics – what a difference a drug makes

'No, I was actually knocked out in the heats, but my sample was identical to the winner's'

Nigel Mansell was mobbed by fans who invaded the pitch – sorry, track – after he won the British
Grand Prix. Less popular figures took note

'Right, Norman, we just sit here and await the adulation of the crowds'

8   Judgement Day

Crime reached record levels in 1992, almost the *Guinness Book of Records* when a defendant committed 274 further offences while on bail. Getting offenders into prison was one thing . . .

'Bail is requested for my client to give him one more chance – he's in striking distance of the record'

. . . Keeping them there was another. The year saw a succession of gaol escapes

'I thought it put a more positive face on the jail escapes, Prime Minister'

After a Broadmoor escape via the washrooms, 'bursting to go' took on a new meaning

The Ablution Block – Broadmoor

Edwina Currie was offered the chance to run the prison service. Her well-known views on eggs, however, were not to everyone's taste

'You can come down now, Smith – she's refused the job'

A highly critical report about Brixton Prison put the Home Secretary, then Kenneth Baker, under some pressure . . .

'Oh dear, Mr Baker, I wasn't expecting you – haven't you been told?'

. . . But he fought back after joyriding hit the headlines. Gangs of youths turned quiet streets into race tracks – Baker was not amused

'Tough? I'll say he's tough!'

'One meets a better class of inmate these days' – the Marquess of Blandford found himself in custody earlier in the year . . .

'. . . And over the centuries the dukes have progressively adopted a more simple form of attire'

. . . Some prison inmates, however, were less aristocratic than others, when it emerged that the party-loving 'Lady Rosemary' had used a bogus title to help her defraud a charity

Lady Mucke's
CHARITY FUND IN AID OF
DUPED CHARITIES

'I wanted to help those more gullible than myself'

1992 saw a spate of audacious 'hole in the wall' raids, as thieves used mechanical diggers as takeaway vehicles

An attempt to rob an art gallery ended in farce when the thieves discovered that their getaway car had been clamped while they were on the job

'I'm afraid we're going to have to call off the chase, Sarge'

Light relief temporarily entered the law courts after a judge was alleged to have made contact with a taxi driver. Why use the long arm of the law when . . .

'Sorry 'bout that, sir – it seems to be suffering what we in BR call Terminal Shock'

'Impressive I grant you, lad, but nothing compared to the great autumn of '83'

TORY MARGINAL AREA AHEAD

PLEASE USE ALTERNATIVE ROUTE

'This is your station announcer: the next Chunnel service will reroute to avoid politically sensitive areas'

'Services could be improved by privatization. Richard Branson wants to start a special rail service . . .'

'Y'know what I miss most – "leaves on the line" '

'Oops! There I go again thinking I'm out on the Atlantic run'

'We were attempting to be the first across the Atlantic in a hot air balloon. Flying at speeds of up to 200 m.p.h. in the jetstream, everything had gone magnificently.

'However, as we were approaching Ireland, we realized it would be dark and that we'd have to fly on. At the speeds we were going, that meant crossing the Russian border at 5.00 a.m.

'I radioed the Russian Embassy.

' "Hello – this is Richard Branson. I'm flying in a balloon across the Atlantic, could I please have permission to cross your border at 5.00 a.m.?"

'A ten-minute wait and then:

' "Mr Branson – I think we can sort this out, which port did you say your ship wanted to come in at?"

'We decided it was safer to ditch than fly on.'

Richard Branson

'Privatizing BR wouldn't be easy, mind'

'My God, Charlie, they're tough negotiators'

'Yup! Had it shipped back lock, stock an' barrel – don't think they've noticed yet'

'And if a private BR fell into foreign hands it could end up in Arizona, like old London Bridge'

'Yup, overcrowding is still a problem – but our customer service teams are working on it . . .'

'It's OK, we're the BR cell not the Lucozade lot – now run, you're free!'

'. . . As I said, BR is getting you there'

'. . . Well, you can take the Fastrack 8.30, the 8.45 RailRocket, the 9.10 Anglo Railrunner or settle for the BR Apology at 9.30'

'Oh dear, there was a time when if you'd made it to the hard shoulder you were
as good as home and dry'

'Speaking as a
roadrunner, things
have become a little
hazardous this
year . . .'

'. . . and fourteen-lane
motorways won't help'

'A huge motorway bridge got stuck while being moved this year. There can be compensation when they move you lock, stock and barrel, mind'

'No, we are not bein' 'elpful, monsieur – we are, how you say, rubbin' eet in'

'. . . While the Germans take advantage of them'

'First the French – now the bloody Germans!'

10   All in the Stars

Larger than life stars were beset by those little problems that affect us all – like the need to diet . . .

'**Mr Pavarotti, if you insist on going on these crash diets at least give your dresser prior notice**'

. . . And the need to establish permanent relationships

'I did, I did, I did, I did, I did, I did, I did . . . I do'

Another little problem for the stars – how to make the best of what nature decided was your lot . . .

'The good news is your new face will withstand the scrutiny of a 500 mm lens
– now, do you want the bad news, Mrs Wobblethorpe?'

. . . And learn to deport yourself with dignity when all about are losing theirs

'It's a modern marriage – neither wears the trousers'

Earlier in the year, the TV franchise holders were criticized for poor programming and told to get their act together . . .

'Derek failed the "quality threshold" test and they revoked his viewing licence'

. . . As were some well-known reporters by irate wives

'. . . And this is Sandy Gall reporting from the dustbin . . .'

Some found escape in 1992, courtesy of Sue Lawley and the Desert Island Marketing Board, which was not all it was cracked up to be . . .

'I can't speak now, darling – all is not what it seems'

. . . Others found no escape. *Blind Date* was spoofed by the PG Tips chimps

'Call me a cynic, but that's where millions of years of evolution gets you – an appearance on
Blind Date!'

It was the end of the turntable for the flared generation when record companies dropped the LP

Entertainment for the year finished on a high note at the Barcelona Olympics

Still, if 1992 was too much you can always hitch a lift into 1993 on a passing Eurofighter